D0690019

21ST CENTURY DEBATES

RAIN FORESTS

OUR IMPACT ON THE PLANET

EWAN McLEISH

RAINTREE
STECK-VAUGHN
RSVP PUBLISHERS

A Harcourt Company

Austin   New York
www.raintreesteckvaughn.com

21st Century Debates Series

Climate Change	Energy Resources	Genetics	Internet
Media	Rain Forests	Surveillance	Waste, Recycling, and Reuse

Published by Raintree Steck-Vaughn Publishers,
an imprint of Steck-Vaughn Company

Library of Congress Cataloging-in-Publication Data
McLeish, Ewan, 1950-
    Rain forests: our impact on the planet/Ewan McLeish.
        p. cm—(21st century debates)
    Includes bibliographical references (p.).
    ISBN 0-7398-3179-8
    1. Rain forests—Juvenile literature. 2. Rain forest ecology—Juvenile
literature. [1. Rain forests. 2. Rain forest ecology. 3. Ecology.] I. Title II. Series.

QH86 .M36 2001
577.34—dc21

00-067335

Printed in Italy. Bound in the United States.
1 2 3 4 5 6 7 8 9 0 LB 06 05 04 03 02

Picture acknowledgments:
Ecoscene 35 (Mike Whittle), 51 (Karl Ammann), 57 (Stephen Coyne),56 (Bruce Harber); Panos Pictures 31 (Giacomo Pirozzi); Popperfoto/Reuters 59; Still Pictures cover foreground and 26 (Mark Edwards), 4 (Heinz Plenge), 5 (Mark Edwards), 7 (Nigel Dickinson), 8 (Nigel Dickinson), 10 (Michael Sewell), 11 (Chafer & Hill), 12 (Chris Caldicott), 13 (Mark Edwards), 14 (Dominique Halleux), 15 (Ron Giling), 16 (Mark Edwards), 17 (Mark Edwards), 18/19 (Tantyo Bangun), 20 (Nigel Dickinson), 22 (Joerg Boethling), 23 (Ron Giling), 25 (Klaus Andrews), 24 (John Maier), 27 (Mark Edwards), 28 (John Maier), 29 (Mark Edwards), 30 (Mark Edwards), 33 (Mark Edwards), 34 (Mike Kolloffel), 36 (Thierry Montford), 37 (Mark Edwards), 38 (Roland Seitre), 39 (Klein/Hubert), 40 (Mark Edwards), 42 (Mike Kolloffel), 43 (Herbert Giradet), 44 (Gerard and Margi Moss), 45 (Roland Seitre), 46 (Nicole Duplaix), 47 (Gilles Nicolet), 48 (Mark Edwards), 49 (Mark Edwards), 50 (Mark Carwardine), 52 (Klein/Hubert-Blois), 53 (Werner Rudhart), 54 (Mark Edwards).

Cover: Foreground picture shows an aerial view of the Amazonian rain forest, Brazil; background picture shows felling a mahogany tree for timber.

CONTENTS

Rain Forests in Danger................................4

Teeming with Life 10

Clearing the Forests 16

Industry—Wealth at a Cost 22

Timber!...26

Peoples of the Rain Forest 34

Sustainable Forests? 40

Can the Rain Forests Survive?............52

Glossary 60

Books, CDs, and Videos.......................61

Useful Addresses..................................62

Index...63

RAIN FORESTS IN DANGER

Some of Our Rain Forests Are Missing

This book is about the world's tropical rain forests, why we are destroying them, and whether it is too late to save them. The word "we" is used deliberately because we are all are involved in their destruction. It follows, therefore, that we can all be involved in helping them to survive.

The world's greatest resource?

Rain forests are often called "the lungs of the world," meaning they play an important part in the control of carbon dioxide and oxygen in the atmosphere. Rain forests also affect the world's climate and stop billions of tons of soil from being washed into the sea. They are the richest wildlife habitats in the world; it is estimated that the Amazon Basin rain forest alone contains more than

This tropical forest in Peru shows the density and variety of plant life typical of rain forests.

10 percent of all known plant and animal species. In addition, rain forests are home to millions of people who have, for thousands of years, lived in harmony with their surroundings and obtained everything they need from beneath its rich canopy.

Rain forests or survival? This forest in Brazil is being destroyed by poor farmers; the road, built by loggers, aids their movement deeper into the forest.

The large-scale destruction of the world's tropical rain forests began about fifty years ago and has been gathering speed ever since. The reasons for this destruction are complicated and sometimes unexpected. They are rooted in poverty and need but also in profit and greed. They are about the treatment of poor countries by rich countries and also about how "we," as individuals, act in our everyday lives.

The effects of destroying the rain forests have often been disastrous and always far-reaching. However, the destruction has not happened without reason. Tropical rain forests provide the countries in which they grow with hugely important resources. These include timber, minerals, and—perhaps most importantly—land. It is the exploitation of these resources that has led to the present situation today.

Difficult questions

The problems facing us in the twenty-first century are whether we can reverse the damage already done to the rain forests and how to conserve those we have left. Or will we simply have to face the fact that any action is too late?

VIEWPOINTS

"From the time of our origins, we have preserved the trees and animals, every single thing in the forest."
Asik, Spokesperson, Penan people, Sarawak, Malaysia

"There is very little we can do. The pressures to remove the forests are too great to be stopped."
Frederic Achard, European Commission Research Center

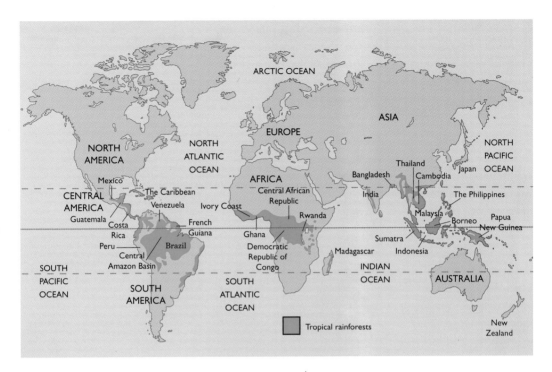

This map shows the location of the Earth's tropical rain forests. These forests once covered twice this area.

Mapping the rain forests

Rain forests stretch in a broad band across the tropical regions of the Earth from Central and South America, through Africa, to Papua New Guinea and North Australia. They cover about 6 percent of the Earth's land surface. Although it is difficult to obtain accurate figures, there is little doubt that rain forests are being destroyed at an ever-increasing rate. Scientific research shows us that mature rain forests once covered at least twice the area they do today. Most of this destruction has happened in the last half of the twentieth century, and almost all of it has been caused by humans.

Rates of destruction differ around the world and occur for different reasons. Improved technology, such as satellite imaging, means that estimates of how much rain forest is being lost are improving all the time. Current data shows that the world is losing an area of rain forest about half the size of Oregon every year.

VIEWPOINT

"If the land as a whole is good, then every part of it is good, whether we understand it or not. Harmony with the land is like harmony with a friend; you cannot cherish his right hand and chop off his left."
*Aldo Leopold,
environmentalist and writer*

Does it matter?

Some people would argue that the survival of rain forests is not important, or is not their concern. Does the survival of a few gorillas in Central Africa or a rare plant in the Philippines really affect our everyday lives? Others argue that everything is connected and that the state of the world's rain forests is an indicator of the health of the planet as a whole. They believe that once we lose more than a certain percentage of forests and wildlife, many other natural systems that sustain us will start to break down.

The Menyah tribe of Borneo are farmers living in harmony with the forest. Since the 1980s they have been protesting against the activities of commercial loggers who threaten their traditional way of life.

FACT

Africa has about 30% of its original forests remaining, Asia 25%, Central America has 50%, and South America 66%. The rain forests of the Amazon Basin are so vast that they gain some protection from their size alone. But at present rates of destruction, even this great area could be halved again in another 50 years.

Cycle of destruction

"Forests come before civilizations, deserts follow them."
Francois-Auguste-René Rodin

Rain forest land may be cleared for small-scale farming, cattle ranching, or a plantation. Trees may be cut down for fuel or timber, or the land may be excavated for minerals. But destroying rain forest is rarely due to one single cause. It is more likely to be a combination of different factors that creates a deadly cycle of destruction. Here is one example:

Burn or starve

A Dayak tribesman from the Indonesian part of Borneo scratches out a living in a rain forest clearing. He does not own the land but simply made his way into the forest along a vast, flattened road left by a logging company. His small patch can hardly support his own family, let alone leave any crops to sell to buy medicines or other essentials. Each year, the thin soil gets poorer. He cannot afford fertilizers and, anyway, they only prolong the life of the soil for a few years before it turns to dust.

Slash and burn. This Brazilian farmer sees no alternative but to burn the forest in order to clear more land for agriculture.

RAIN FORESTS IN DANGER

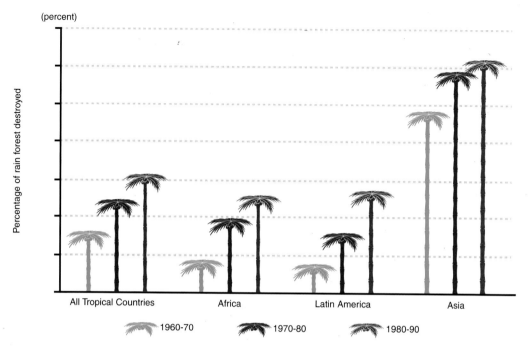

(percent)

Percentage of rain forest destroyed

All Tropical Countries   Africa   Latin America   Asia

1960-70   1970-80   1980-90

He has two alternatives. One is to clear more land by setting fire to the nearby forest. The other is to starve. It is not much of a choice, but it is an easy one to make. He burns the forest.

This, on its own, does not seem so bad. The forests of Southeast Asia are still huge, and the farmer is not a greedy man. Unfortunately there are many like him, all equally poor and all equally desperate, so they burn the forest, too. Soon there are many fires blazing in the forest. Some get out of control. Others are started deliberately by plantation owners who see the opportunity to clear more land in order to grow oil palms, pineapples, and bananas to sell to rich developed countries in the West.

Situations such as these often seem to be a choice between people and the environment. Can we really expect people to have "long-term vision" when they are starving?

During the past decade (1990–2000) rain forest destruction worldwide has remained at least as high as 1990 levels and is higher in some countries, such as Sumatra and parts of Borneo (Indonesia).

DEBATE

Who is really to blame for destroying the rain forest? The farmer who started the fire? The loggers who stripped much of the existing forest? The plantation owners for cashing in? Do you think it is the fault of the Indonesian government for failing to control the situation?

TEEMING WITH LIFE

A jaguar in a tropical forest in Belize; like many large rain forest animals, the jaguar is an endangered species.

Struggling to Survive

Rain forests are unique habitats. They contain the greatest number and biodiversity of living things on Earth. But it is not just the variety of life that makes rain forests so important. They are home to many of the world's most endangered species. The mountain gorilla is struggling to survive in the Central African rain forests of Congo and Rwanda, and the future of the golden lion tamarin hangs by a thread in Brazil's Atlantic rain forest. The Central American country of Costa Rica has 16 endangered mammal species, 13 of which live in safety in the country's Amistad Biosphere Reserve. Like the gorilla, the South American orangutan is now an endangered species, and it is likely that these, two of humanity's closest living relatives, could become extinct in the wild in our lifetime.

Twenty percent of all bird species are found in the Amazonian rain forests, including the Amazonian toucan.

Dwindling numbers

It is estimated that the number of living species on Earth could be anything between 5 and 15 million. It is impossible to put a figure on the exact number, because so many are either unknown or unnamed. Most unknown species are insects or other tiny animals and plants. It is further estimated that between 50 percent and 90 percent of these live in tropical rain forests. At the present rates of forest loss, 4 to 8 percent of rain forest species could be extinct by 2015 and 17 to 35 percent by 2040. This could mean the extinction of 20 to 75 species per day. Although most will be small invertebrates, they form the base of an interconnected web that supports the rain forest and ultimately life on Earth.

VIEWPOINTS

"Destroying rain forests and the species they contain for short-term gain is like burning down an ancient library before you read the books."
Edward O. Wilson, Biologist and writer

"Many people have suffered massive economic hardship. Trees are ... the easiest way to make money quickly."
Rudi Syaf, Conservation Information Forum, Sumatra

Rain forests play an important role in regulating climate and weather patterns: When forests are cleared, less moisture can evaporate, creating less rainfall.

Life support

Rain forests are vital to the Earth's well-being. The trees take up the huge amounts of rainfall through their roots and return to the atmosphere through their leaves, which creates the wet, tropical rain forest climate. When large areas of forest are cleared, the climate changes and becomes drier. The soil, held in place by a network of interlocking tree roots, is rapidly blown or washed away. During heavy rainstorms, rain forests act like giant sponges, soaking up the water and preventing flooding. This is vital in regions where most of the rain falls at one time of year, such as during the monsoon season in Bangladesh.

Global warming?

Rain forests also regulate the amount of carbon dioxide (CO_2) in the atmosphere and release huge amounts of oxygen. They are therefore important in controlling the composition of the air we breathe and the "greenhouse effect" or global warming. Cutting down or burning forests releases huge amounts of carbon dioxide into the atmosphere, which increases global temperatures.

A thousand uses

Rain forests not only support an incredible variety of wild animals and plants, but they also support human beings and their communities. Millions of people still inhabit the rain forests and depend on them for everything they need, from food and clothing to ropes and medicines.

Many of our common cultivated food plants, such as rice, tea, chocolate, bananas, and coffee, originally came from wild rain forest plants. Now, genes from rain forest plants can be used to improve the resistance of cultivated crops to pests or disease. For example, a wild coffee species from Ethiopia's threatened rain forests was used to save crops throughout Latin America from disease. Rubber, resins, waxes, edible oils, nuts and fruits, dyes and flavorings, gum, tannins (used in leather and ink production), rattan palms (used for ropes and fibers), bamboo, pesticides, and lubricants are all rain forest products. Rubber exports alone earn more than $3 billion annually for tropical countries and rattan earns $4 billion.

VIEWPOINTS

"Our success depends on how well we can understand, control, and manage the Earth's life-support systems for our benefit."
Planetary Management Worldview

"Our massive tampering with the world's interdependent web of life—coupled with the environmental damage inflicted by deforestation, species loss, and climate change—could trigger widespread catastrophic effects."
Letter to the world's leaders by 1,680 leading scientists, 1992

Destroying forests means that the soil is no longer protected from the rain. The resulting erosion forms deep gullies, with the result that water runs off the land more rapidly.

Medicine chest

In the early sixteenth century, European explorers
returned from South America with the dried bark
of the cinchona tree. They had seen how the local
Indian population used it to cure fever. The bark
contained quinine, the chemical substance that, to
this day, is the most effective treatment for malaria
yet discovered. Since that time, thousands of
medicines have been developed from rain forest
plants, often with the help of the indigenous
(native) people.

Rain forest health service

The active ingredients for 25 percent of the world's
medicines are substances that come from plants.
Over 2,000 tropical rain forest plants have been
identified that may help fight cancer, and over 120
pure chemical substances, used in hundreds of

*Medicine for the picking. The rosy
periwinkle, being harvested here in
Madagascar, contains a substance that
is used in a successful treatment for
leukemia, a form of cancer.*

medicines, come from rain forest species. They include diosgenin, from which the contraceptive pill was developed, made from a wild yam found in Mexico and Guatemala; tubocurarine, used as a muscle-relaxant during surgery, made from the Amazonian liana; and a substance extracted from the rosy periwinkle, which treats leukemia. Animals can also provide medicine—the poisonous spur of the South American armadillo has been used to develop anti-leprosy drugs.

Cocoa arriving at Amsterdam, the Netherlands, from the Ivory Coast. If rich countries paid higher prices for rain forest products such as these, the need to clear more forest land for plantations would be reduced.

Touching our lives

Rain forests touch the daily lives of everyone on Earth. In addition to thousands of medicines they supply half of the world's annual harvest of hardwood; thousands of foods, such as cocoa and tropical fruits; and hundreds of natural products such as latex rubber and vegetable oils. Scientists believe that many more new cures, new foods, and other products await discovery. By destroying rain forests we are destroying a resource that sustains us.

DEBATE

With modern technologies, do we really need to rely on finding "wonder drugs" and other useful products in the rain forests? Do we only value animals and plants because they are useful to us? Is it right, therefore, to preserve some species but not others?

CLEARING THE FORESTS

The Vanishing Soil

The spread of poor settlers onto rain forest land is probably the biggest single cause of tropical rain forest destruction. Most of it is unplanned and unregulated, but some of it is deliberate. It is tempting for governments with overcrowded cities and high concentrations of population to set up "transmigration programs" and move people to so-called underpopulated areas.

These migrants have been moved by the Indonesian government from Java to Sumatra. In order to survive, they have burned down the forest near their shack to grow food.

Since the 1970s, Indonesia has moved large numbers of people and resettled them in its numerous outer islands. In the 1970s and 1980s, Brazil also moved thousands of people from the ghettos and shantytowns of its big cities to the forested areas of the Rondoñia region. But there was no employment for the migrants—all they could do was attempt to farm. The results have spelled disaster for the rain forest.

No nutrients

It is natural to think that forest soils are rich and productive. This is true in the case of the drier, more temperate woods and forests found at higher latitudes in the world. But tropical rain forests are different, because most of the nutrients are stored in the trees and plants themselves.

In a rain forest, when leaves and branches fall to the ground, the warm temperatures and wet conditions cause them to decompose incredibly quickly. Insects, such as termites and other invertebrates, break the leaves down into small pieces. Then bacteria and fungi reduce them still further into microscopic nutrients. These are immediately taken up by trees and other plants so they are recycled back into the rain forest itself. The soil never has the chance to build up into a thick, rich layer.

The Talang Mamak people of Sumatra grow traditional corn as a food crop. Their way of life—and the rain forest itself—is threatened by forest clearance for oil palm plantations.

VIEWPOINT

"The solution to poverty and overcrowding is to match the people with no land to the land with no people."
Brazilian government policy

17

FACT

Estimates put the area of forest destroyed by fire in Indonesia in 1997 at between 370,000 and 742,000 acres (150,000 and 300,000 ha)— equivalent to a 1 mile-wide strip of forest stretching for 1,864 miles (3,000 km). In Brazil, the rate of deforestation each year may be as high as 7.4 million acres (3 million ha).

In 1997 huge areas of Indonesian rain forest were destroyed by fire. And every year more and more forests burn. Once destroyed it is unlikely that they will ever recover.

Slash and burn

Much of the agriculture in rain forest areas is what is called shifting cultivation. Since tropical forest soils are poor, farming depends on nutrients released from the trees themselves when the forest is burned. The burned area is farmed for a time and then left to recover. Such cultivation has been going on for thousands of years with little damage to the rain forest ecosystem. But with increasing numbers of settlers, the forest cannot recover, and the fragile soil rapidly becomes exhausted. The only alternative for the farmer is to move on and cut down or burn more forest to gain a few more years' survival. This cycle of destruction is known as "slash and burn."

Fire in the sky

Fire is one of the greatest threats to forests. Of course, fires occur naturally, caused by a stray bolt of lightning for example. They spread quickly across the rain forest floor, doing relatively little

damage to the high canopy above and giving birds and animals the chance to escape.

In October 1997, satellites high over the Pacific Ocean sent back their usual pictures of the giant series of islands named Indonesia. But this time, something seemed to be wrong. Dotted over the islands were thousands of "hot spots"—points of light. At first, scientists could not believe what they were seeing. It looked as if Indonesia was in flames.

A lethal killer

For a tropical country such as Indonesia, the climate had been particularly dry that year. A change in the world's ocean currents, known as El Niño, had caused the rains to fall farther east. Indonesia's rain forests were bone-dry and ready to burn. But the change in climate was not the real cause of the inferno—the fires had been started deliberately by people living in such poverty that they had no alternative but to burn the forests in order to survive.

VIEWPOINTS

"Fire is good. Burning the land means we'll all have enough food to fill our bellies for the year. Fire is life."
Abdur Rani, Dayak tribesman and farmer

"Local people know that the water levels are dropping in their rice fields and that it's because of the forest disappearing. But they and the government only think in the short term. There is no long-term vision."
Susi Lawaty, WWF field officer, Kerinci-Seblat National Park, Sumatra

A black desert

The fires eventually burned themselves out, helped by a change in wind direction, rainfall, the efforts of firefighters, and the fact that there was simply nothing left to burn. Gigantic rain forest trees will never grow there again, and the land will change for good. Before long, poor families will arrive. They will plant crops for a few years before moving on; or companies will buy up the land and create plantations of palm oil or fast-growing trees; then

Cattle ranching results in whole areas of forest being cleared. Then the cattle cause more damage as they munch away at the remaining forest edges.

cattle and goats may be moved in to graze, nibbling away at the edges of remaining forest. The rain forest is making way for a different world.

Home on the range

Damage in rain forest areas is also caused by grazing livestock. Often, the land that has been damaged already by farmers, who can no longer grow crops on it, is sold to ranchers who can afford to fertilize the soil so that grass grows for a few years. However, the end result is usually the same— chemical or artificial fertilizers add nutrients to the soil but do not hold it together. Only the addition of more vegetable matter can do that. Before long, the soil turns to dust, helped now by the churning hooves of thousands of cattle.

Cattle invaders

Some of the worst examples of damage are in India. In the past, cattle farmers here were often nomadic, moving their herds to areas where the grazing was good and then moving on before the land suffered. Now, the spread of more permanent agriculture has forced the farmers into the rain forest margins, where the cattle destroy the forest edges and gradually move deeper into the rain forest itself. India has 400 million cattle, and it is estimated that 90 million live on rain forest land.

Burgers for trees

In Central America, livestock ranching has also contributed massively to forest destruction. In Brazil in the 1970s and 1980s, landowners were encouraged to raise cattle on forested land in exchange for tax incentives. Selling cattle abroad, particularly to the United States for beef, brought in important foreign income for the government. But the result of this policy was such widespread destruction of rain forests that it has now been stopped.

FACT

Burning rain forests to make way for ranching still remains an enormous problem. In Kalimantan and Sabah, in the Indonesian part of Borneo, 15,445 square miles (40,000 sq. km, an area twice the size of New Jersey) were lost in one year.

DEBATE

Can you blame poor governments with over-populated cities for clearing slums and sending people where land is plentiful? What else might these poor governments have done? Are settlers powerless victims, or do they have some control over their situation?

INDUSTRY—
WEALTH AT A COST

Is It Worth It?

In all countries, industry is an important way of creating wealth, but the wealth often comes at a price. Europe's space program, based in French Guiana, South America, is powered by hydro-electric energy provided by a massive dam. A 227-mile (365-km) stretch of rain forest was flooded when the dam was built, and the submerged vegetation now produces more greenhouse gases than several fossil-fuel power plants. Estimates put the amounts at 21 tons of carbon dioxide and methane a year for every person living in this small country. That will be a total of 66 million tons of greenhouse gases over the next twenty years.

Power to the people

While it is unusual for a dam to power a space program, many developing countries build dams to provide power for industry or electricity for thousands of towns and villages. Water is plentiful in tropical countries, which often have few other energy sources, so it makes sense that their governments decide to use the water to generate electricity.

The top of this temple is the tip of a village flooded by the construction of the Sardar Sarovar Dam, Gujarat, India.

However, dam building can bring many disadvantages. In addition to flooding vast areas of forest, people are driven from their land, and the flooded areas often breed diseases such as malaria. Some hydro-electric dams are used to power large industrial processes such as aluminum smelting or steel production. These in turn cause further damage to the land. Industry brings economic benefits and employment to an area, but the industries themselves may create more problems for the rain forest.

The Narmada River Scheme in India is the world's largest current hydroelectric power and irrigation project. The project involves building 30 major dams over a period of 50 years. It will irrigate 7,722 square miles (20,000 sq km) of land in the states of Gujarat and Madhya Pradesh, provide drinking water for the whole region, and generate enough power to develop new industries and bring electricity to most of the villages in the area. The scheme was started in 1987 but was held up between 1995 and 1999 due to protests by local conservation groups. It has now resumed again with only minor modifications.

This giant excavator at a bauxite mine in Suriname tears through thousands of tons of soil and rock an hour to mine aluminum ore.

Small is beautiful?

For many years, Western governments and international bodies, such as the World Bank, have been lending money to poorer developing countries for dam-building schemes. They see this as a way of making the countries more self-reliant and also of winning important construction contracts for Western companies. But the idea that "bigger is better" has now changed. It has been realized that building more much smaller dams causes less disruption to people and less damage to the environment. Another advantage is that a small dam can supply electricity to a local area where it is needed most.

Death in the water. This miner uses mercury to separate gold from sediment in the Madeira River, Amazonia. By doing so he not only endangers his own life, but also all those who use the river as a source of food.

Mining the forests

Rainforest areas are often rich in precious minerals, such as silver and gold. However, mining can severely damage the rain forest environment: Vast areas must be cleared and access roads built. Water courses can be damaged, and heavy machinery flattens and compacts the soil.

Hidden killer

In gold mining, mercury is used to extract raw gold from mine waste. When a miner inhales mercury vapor it attacks the brain, causing uncontrollable shaking, a fear of bright light, and eventual blindness.

In the Amazon region, even people who live hundreds of miles from mining sites suffer. This is because the mercury gets into water paths where it collects in the sediments and is almost impossible to remove. It passes up the food chain and eventually accumulates in fish. The local people eat the fish and are poisoned.

Scientists have suggested that local people should eat only herbivorous fish, since the mercury inside them is less concentrated than in the carnivorous species farther up the food chain. It is not much of a choice.

Made in Japan

Rain forests are not only rich in precious metals but also in minerals such as aluminum and iron ore. One of the largest international projects in the Amazon region is the Carajas Iron Ore Scheme, jointly financed by the World Bank, the EU (European Union), and Japan. It has resulted in the conversion of an area of rain forest the size of France to industrial and agricultural use. The iron produced by the project is exported for car manufacture in Japan and Europe.

The metal used in these cars may have been mined deep in the rain forest.

DEBATE

Mining and industry bring wealth to poor countries. How can poor countries gain the benefit of industrial development without destroying rain forests, and what might be the role of the wealthier countries in helping them to achieve this?

TIMBER!

Logs for Sale

R ain forest trees are one of the most valuable exports for developing countries. Tropical hardwood is prized around the world for its strength, beauty, and durability. A single rain forest tree can be worth over $1,000, and developing countries make over $8 billion annually from selling hardwoods overseas.

Trees are made into sawwood (planks), plywood (thin layers), and veneers (very thin layers placed on top of cheaper woods). These are used to construct buildings, ships, railroad sleepers, furniture, luxury cars and boats, all kinds of household goods, games, toys, and musical instruments. Some wood is turned into pulp for packaging and paper-making.

Cutting down this mahogany tree is only the first step in the destruction of a rain forest. The logging roads will be quickly colonized by poor farmers who will clear more land.

Log leagues

The rate at which trees are being cut down for timber is increasing. This is happening mostly in Southeast Asia, which supplies nearly 75 percent of all exported tropical timber, much of it to Japan. Africa is the next largest exporter. Timber production in South America is mostly for home use, but this may change as Asian supplies run out.

Widespread damage

Logging has already led to some trees coming close to extinction. Loggers want only the best wood, so they concentrate on a few valuable species. However, these can be so widely scattered that many other trees may be damaged or destroyed in the felling process. More are damaged by heavy machinery as the chosen trees are dragged away. In all, extracting a few prime trees per acre may result in damage to over half of those that remain. In addition, the access roads built to transport the logs away from the forest become entry routes for landless farmers and the homeless poor.

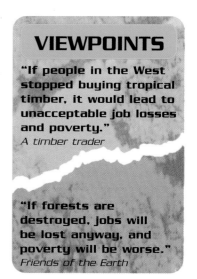

VIEWPOINTS

"If people in the West stopped buying tropical timber, it would lead to unacceptable job losses and poverty."
A timber trader

"If forests are destroyed, jobs will be lost anyway, and poverty will be worse."
Friends of the Earth

Furniture made from the tropical hardwood rattan, being taken to market in Thailand. The furniture generates local income, but it is unlikely the rattan trees will be replaced.

Plant more trees?

One answer could be to plant trees specifically for timber production. Between 1980 and 1995, the number of forest plantations, mostly in Southeast Asia, increased to 247 million acres (100 million ha.) However, plantation forests are usually poor in biodiversity compared to original rain forest. Sometimes, original rain forest is actually removed in order to plant faster-growing varieties.

This road will link Manaus in Brazil with Boa Vista in Venezuela. Each new road improves communications but divides the rain forest into smaller sections.

FACT

Even where forests are not totally destroyed, their biodiversity may be badly affected as certain important tree species, such as mahogany, are removed. These types of forests are not included in statistics for forest destruction.

Mahogany—a road to nowhere

Broadleaf mahogany is found in a wide band across southern Amazonia. It stretches over four regions: Pará, Mato Grosso, Rondoñia, and Acre. The United Kingdom buys 85 percent of its mahogany from here and the United States is also a major buyer. After more than twenty years of heavy logging, mahogany is almost extinct in the eastern part of the region. The logging is now moving steadily westward. A fifth of the mahogany zone is covered by reserves set aside for the indigenous people, but because the trees are more numerous in the reserves, they are constant targets for illegal logging.

Mahogany trees grow widely spaced apart, and to harvest them a vast network of roads must be built through the rain forests. Once the roads have been built, settlers are able to move in more easily and clear the forest for cattle. This drives away game, resulting in a poor diet among the Indians. In the south of Pará, 1,864 miles (3,000 km) of roads have penetrated Indian reserves and other such protected areas.

The human cost

The incoming people bring new diseases, to which the Indians have little resistance. In 1995 the Kayapo tribe suffered a steep rise in malaria, tuberculosis, and other lung diseases as a result of contact with miners and loggers. Other diseases, as well as alcoholism and mercury pollution, also rose dramatically.

In an effort to protect the Indians, the Brazilian government encourages them to abandon their semi-nomadic way of life and live in permanent settlements. Often they cannot find or grow enough food. The result is that they are more likely to accept bribes and sign illegal contracts for wood or mining rights. This sets up tensions within the tribes between the older leaders, who want to keep their traditional lands, and younger members who see the timber companies as a way out of poverty and the old way of life.

The construction of Route BR 364 brought pressures from the outside world to the Surui tribe in Brazil, changing their way of life forever.

VIEWPOINTS

"The lands traditionally occupied by the Indians are set aside for their permanent possession, leaving to them the exclusive use of the riches from the soil, the rivers, and the lakes."
Brazilian Constitution 1988

"They (the loggers) steal the wood secretly. It's ours. They come in, cut the timber, take it out and sell it for themselves. We're left with nothing."
Tigaro Arara. Arara tribe. Pará. Brazil

This giant blast furnace in Carajas turns iron ore into pig iron. It is used in Brazil's developing industries or exported abroad. The furnace is fueled by charcoal, made from Amazon forest trees, and the project is funded by the World Bank.

Wood—the fuel of the poor

For many millions of people living in the tropics, the only source of fuel for cooking and heating is wood. This is collected either directly, or converted into charcoal and sold in the cities or wherever wood is no longer available. For example, charcoal produced in the forests of northern Thailand finds a good market in the deforested regions of Bangladesh. Charcoal is also used as an industrial fuel, such as in steel production in Brazil, on a scale that causes local rain forest areas to be destroyed.

Supply and demand

In many parts of the world today, the demand for fuelwood far exceeds supply. Over 2 billion people have difficulty finding enough to meet their most basic needs, while the impact on the environment is obvious. Between 7,700 and 9,700 square miles (20,000 and 25,000 sq km) of forest and woodland are cleared annually for fuelwood.

Health and nutrition

There is also a human cost to this shortage. For example, when boiling water becomes an unaffordable luxury, disease quickly follows. Some parents are also forced to feed their children on quick-cooking cereals rather than slower-cooking, more nutritious foods such as beans. Nearly two-thirds of Rwanda's people have only enough fuel to cook one meal a day, while many of the remainder cannot even afford this luxury.

Even in wood-rich areas such as the Amazon, there are local wood shortages. In Manaus, Brazil, most poor people depend on charcoal for cooking, but as the forest recedes, the price keeps rising due to increased transport costs. The only alternative is an exhausting two- or three-hour daily trek to fetch wood. In the Democratic Republic of Congo, the time spent collecting wood to meet a family's needs is equivalent to 250 to 300 days a year.

> **FACT**
>
> Fuelwood provides 58% of the energy consumed in Africa, 17% in Asia and 8% in Central and South America. More than 90% of energy-use in nations such as the Democratic Republic of Congo comes from wood. It even supplies four-fifths of the energy needed in oil-rich Nigeria. Overall, one-third of the world's population depends on it.

This girl from Niger is relieved to have found wood for the family cooking. But as the forest recedes, the daily trek will become longer.

When wealth meets poverty

Logging is big business. It would be surprising if countries with forests did not look for ways to exploit them. In Europe almost all of the original, temperate forests have already been destroyed.

However, most tropical counties do attempt to manage their forests. After all, they do not wish to see a resource that brings in so much foreign capital destroyed. In Indonesia, for example, there are 350 million acres (143 million hectares) of rain forest, of which 158 million acres (64 million ha) are "production forest." In practice, this means that loggers are permitted to take five to ten trees with a 20-inch (50-cm) diameter from each acre. 120 million acres (49 million ha) are protected and cannot be logged. The remaining 74 million acres (30 million ha) are known as "conversion land," or land that can be converted to agriculture.

This chart shows the biggest threats to tropical rain forests throughout the world. As you can see, the main threats vary from region to region.

Threats to tropical rain forests

Region	Original forest under threat	Threatened forest at risk from:				
		Logging	Mining, roads, etc.	Cleared for agriculture	Cleared for other uses	Other causes*
Africa	77%	79%	12%	17%	8%	41%
Asia	60%	50%	10%	20%	9%	24%
South America	54%	69%	53%	32%	14%	5%
Europe**	100%	80%	0%	0%	20%	0%
World	39%	72%	38%	20%	14%	13%

*Other causes include plantations, fire, and the splitting of forests into smaller fragments.

** Europe is included for comparison; these are not rain forests.

Note: The percentage risks add up to more than 100 percent, since forests may be threatened by more than one factor.

Although this may sound reasonable, the reality is often very different. In countries as vast and as poor as Indonesia, the authorities are often powerless to stop illegal logging. Poorly paid officials may be easily bribed by the logging companies to turn a blind eye to their illegal activities. For those higher in authority—even in government—there is less excuse. Many have financial interests in logging companies or paper mills.

VIEWPOINT

"There's politics, there's greed, there's corruption, there's poverty. We can make some progress, but all we can do is hold back the forest destruction. We can't stop it."
Raleigh Blouch, World Bank, Kerinci-Seblat National Park, Sumatra

The wood at this timber mill in Sumatra has been felled illegally. Once sawed into planks, however, it will be impossible to trace.

DEBATE

Can people in the West criticize developing countries for exploiting their own resources? Are rain forests such a valuable global resource that they should be considered as belonging to "the world" rather than to individual nations? If so, what responsibility do wealthy nations have in helping countries with rain forests make better use of them?

PEOPLES OF THE RAIN FOREST

A Need to Weep

Perhaps the greatest casualties of rain forest destruction are the original peoples who inhabited them. Indigenous tribes were once common throughout the world's rain forests. Each tribe had its own culture, language, and way of life, largely cut off from outside influences. The decline of many indigenous nations began when colonists arrived from other countries during the sixteenth and seventeenth centuries. The most recent decline has happened over the last thirty years, coinciding with widespread rain forest exploitation.

An Indian family in Ecuador traveling by river. Traditional ways of life are rapidly being lost as rain forests are destroyed.

Today, in the Amazon region alone, the remaining indigenous peoples speak 180 different languages, but their numbers are down to 150,000. One tribe, the Tikuna, is the second largest Indian group left in Brazil. In 1988, the Brazilian government set aside 741,000 acres (300,000 ha) for them, but timber cutters, angry at the loss of "their" land, shot and killed a number of the Indians. Now, the Indians live in fear and are afraid to roam through the rain forest that was set aside for them. Instead, they survive by fishing and tending small patches of land in government settlements or rain forest towns.

Changes to the rain forest can sometimes bring benefits such as better education. But, more often, promised results such as new schools and jobs never appear.

Vanishing tribes

The Penan people live in the rain forests of Malaysia. They were once nomadic hunters and gatherers, who had lived entirely off the plants and animals of the rain forest for centuries. In the late twentieth century, huge Japanese freighters came to fill their ships with timber from the forest, and the people's lives changed forever.

As the trees fell, the Penan drifted toward settlements built for them by the government. At first the new way of life seemed a bearable alternative, with its promises of health care, education, and employment. However, the schools and clinics that were promised were never built and there were few jobs except for laboring in the logging camps. Without the rain forest to support them, the people began to fall into poverty and apathy. Today, no more than 300 out of 7,000 Penan live in the old ways.

VIEWPOINT

"Once we were great warriors. Now we struggle to protect our land. We must hold on to our land and culture. We can never give these up."
Pedro Inacio Pinheiro, Village captain, Tikuna tribe, Brazil

A gold mine in French Guiana attracts workers from outside the area. The result may be disease and destruction of the way of life for local people.

Alien invasion

When indigenous people come into contact with the outside world, it is hardly surprising that the consequences are often disastrous for the native population. In the Amazon region in the 1980s, gold prospectors and *garimpeiros* (miners) flocked to the forested regions of Rondoñia, Pará, and Mato Grosso in search of a fortune.

One consequence of this invasion was that large areas of rain forest were cut down to open up mining sites. Another is that "tailing" (waste from gold mining) has damaged the fragile forest eco-system. Panning for gold in the rain forest streams and rivers has destroyed banks and created stagnant, swamplike ponds—ideal breeding grounds for malaria-carrying mosquitoes.

The mosquitoes quickly spread malaria through the makeshift mining towns. The *garimpeiros* have little resistance to the disease, and the correct treatment is hard to come by. Today, new drug-resistant strains of malaria are taking hold, and the indigenous people themselves, previously naturally resistant to malaria, are falling victim to the disease.

Culture clash

In 1987, *garimpeiros* invaded the homeland of 10,000 Yanomami Indians in northern Brazil and southern Venezuela. Within two years, 40,000 miners were working on their land. Violent clashes took place between the angry Yanomami and the miners, but there was worse to come. The Indians fell victim to many previously unknown diseases carried by the miners, such as measles and influenza. In addition to disease, the miners also introduced alcohol, tobacco, television, and new foods to a people whose way of life had stayed unchanged for centuries.

The overall consequence is that many indigenous peoples are caught between two cultures. They cannot go back to the old ways but they also cannot adapt to the more "Westernized" way of life of the new immigrants. Unemployment, alcoholism, and suicide are often high among indigenous groups who have lost their identity along with their land.

VIEWPOINT

"Bulldozers and roads destroy familiar features. The land becomes unrecognizable, producing a sort of collective amnesia (forgetfulness about the past)."
Dr. Peter Brosius, anthropologist, University of Georgia

A young Yanomami woman, ill with malaria, is carried to the doctor's plane to be taken to a hospital. Clearing rain forests can damage rivers and increase numbers of malaria-carrying mosquitoes.

A group of botanists returns from research in the rain forests of Madagascar. The more we know about rain forests and the people they support, the better we will be able to protect them.

VIEWPOINTS

"In the past, the two (people and tigers) could live together but now the area is no longer big enough to support both of them. Allowing the people to stay means dooming them to poverty— and the tigers to extinction."
Dr. John Robinson, Director, Nagarole National Park, India

"Conservation groups think they know the answers to the problems and that they should be making decisions, but it is wrong. I personally think that in many countries it is impossible and unfair to stop the use of forests for the benefit of local people."
Gonzales Oviedo, World Wide Fund for Nature

West is best?

It is easy for those in the developed West to think they know what is best on matters of rain forest conservation. But it is important to try not to impose ideas without properly consulting the local people or respecting their traditions.

In 1990, on the West Samoan Island of Savii in the Pacific, a European conservation organization was asked to help local people resist the advances of a big logging company by encouraging other forms of income. At first, the project went well. An agreement was signed to build a new school and to set up a 12,350-acre (5,000-ha) rain forest reserve. There were plans for a solar power plant and a tourist wildlife center.

Then money for the project went to fund expensive offices in the capital, rather than to the villages, and local people were not consulted on important decisions. Gradually, an atmosphere of mistrust arose, and in 1993 the project was abandoned. A reconciliation has since occurred, and today the local people have set up their own plan to protect the rain forest.

A difference of opinion

In India, conservationists and the local population are currently battling over a different clash of ideas. The director of the Nagarole National Park believes the only way to preserve 40 rare Asian tigers is to move 6,000 people from their homes in the park. The problem is that some of the people are illegally hunting deer, the tigers' natural prey. He thinks that anyone who argues that the indigenous people should stay has a romantic view of these people and their way of life and is denying them a better life elsewhere.

Hunter hunted? The Asian tiger is endangered throughout its range because of poaching and extermination of its prey, such as deer.

DEBATE

Is the notion that indigenous people live in harmony with their surroundings and are part of the balance of nature just a romantic idea held by the West? In an age where "Western" values are widespread, is it realistic for indigenous people to go on living in traditional ways, especially if they remain poor or may endanger the environment?

SUSTAINABLE FORESTS?

Why Forests Are Destroyed

"Human beings are…entitled to a healthy and productive life in harmony with nature."
Principle 1, Rio Declaration on
Environment and Development

We have been looking at the causes of rain forest destruction, the greatest of which is fire to clear land for farming. The demand for land has meant that the number of fires has increased in recent years, and rain forests can no longer recover as they once did. Farmers sell exhausted land to plantation owners or ranchers who try and obtain more land and often cause more damage. More rain forest is destroyed due to the demand for wood, both for timber and firewood. Mining, other industries, and dam-building account for further forest destruction. Often, competing claims on the rain forest lead to conflict between different

As long as activities such as this illegal tin mine in the Amazon Basin are allowed to carry on, rain forest destruction will continue.

groups, especially between outside developers and indigenous people, who often suffer as a result.

The population question

The causes of rain forest destruction are so vast and so complex, it seems impossible to know how they can be tackled. One way is to attack the underlying cause—what do you think this is?

If you came up with poverty (or something similar, such as lack of jobs or opportunities) then you are pretty close. Of course, you could argue that population growth is the main cause—if fewer people lived in these countries, there wouldn't be this problem. This is true, but only to an extent. A single logging company does far more damage to a rain forest than do several thousand people. Remember also that it is mainly people in the West who benefit from logging, mining, and plantations.

It is true that slash-and-burn agriculture is probably the biggest single cause of rain forest destruction. But it is poverty and landlessness, rather than over-population, that create poor farmers. They do not choose to be poor or to destroy their environment, but they lack the equipment and the training to do a better job. Although population is clearly a factor in rain forest destruction, poverty is the main cause.

Tackling poverty

How do you tackle poverty? It means finding fairer ways to treat people by giving better prices for produce, such as crops and timber, sold abroad. It also means creating better conditions—providing all people the right to basic needs, such as employment, education, health, and justice. It has been proved that when people have decent living conditions, they are less likely to damage their environment. To achieve this, people need to be given more responsibility for their lives—and for the land.

VIEWPOINTS

"If current predictions of population growth on the planet remain unchanged, science and technology may not be able to prevent either irreversible degradation of the environment or continued poverty for much of the world."
U.S. National Academy of Sciences and the Royal Society of London, 1992

"People tend to have fewer and healthier children, and live longer when they have access to education, jobs.... and when they live in societies where their individual rights are respected."
G. Tyler Miller, Professor of Human Ecology

FACT

Japan imports more tropical timber than all other countries put together. Most of this is in the form of raw logs, from which the exporting countries get relatively little benefit.

A question of development

"Protection of the environment shall be part of development and cannot be considered in isolation from it."
Principle 4, Rio Declaration on Environment and Development

Today, all developing countries, many of which are in rain forest areas, are changing rapidly. They are becoming industrialized societies just as the developed countries in the West did two or three centuries earlier. We cannot stop this process, nor should we try. But it may be possible to influence that development and, at the same time, learn from the mistakes of the past. This is the only way that rain forests will survive.

What is development?
Development is really about how we use the world's resources like land, minerals, water, and forests. In June 1992, most of the world's leaders held a meeting, the Earth Summit, in Rio de Janeiro, Brazil. They met to discuss how these resources could be developed in ways that are sustainable. This means that resources should be

Sustainable development means that this poor family in Acre, Brazil, should be able to enjoy a decent standard of living without destroying their environment.

able to meet the needs of people now but still be available for use by future generations.

Leaders at the Earth Summit in 1992 pledged to work together for sustainable development. The problems of rain forest destruction can only be tackled with international cooperation.

One of the outcomes of the Earth Summit was the Rio Declaration on Environment and Development. Two of the principles from this declaration are found at the top of page 40 and the page opposite. You will notice that they are about people as well as the environment. Principle 1 goes on to state that:

> "Human beings are at the center of concerns for sustainable development."

In other words, environmental problems such as the destruction of the rain forests cannot be considered without also considering human issues and concerns.

Turning the tide

What does sustainable development mean for rain forests? Is it realistic to think that they can be used to meet human needs without being destroyed in the process? On the following pages, you can read examples of sustainable approaches to rain forests. Think about the issues they raise.

Once these bare mountain slopes in Madagascar were clothed in trees. Now efforts are being made to save Madagascar's remaining rain forests.

VIEWPOINT

"But if you want people to help preserve the forest, it's not enough to simply fence it off and throw away the key. You've got to offer them better ways to make a living."
Koto Bernard, Madagascan scientist

Masoala National Park, Madagascar

Madagascar, an island off the east coast of Africa, contains some of the richest and most diverse lowland and coastal rain forest in the world. It has been cut off from the mainland for millions of years, so many of its plants and animals are found nowhere else. Over the years, much of its rain forest has been damaged by logging and land clearance. But now the situation is changing, and the government of Madagascar is working with international organizations to improve matters.

A number of national parks have been set up to protect the rain forests, including the Masoala National Park on the northeast coast. At first, the local people feared they would no longer be allowed to cut down trees or sell hardwoods.

However, the park rangers showed them how to use the forest's resources more wisely and created special buffer zones where trees could still be harvested and land farmed. Whenever trees are cut down, more are planted to replace them.

On the park's eastern border, one village is launching a "green" timber industry. They will harvest rare hardwoods in their buffer zone and sell the timber to overseas companies who only use environmentally sensitive methods.

As a result of taking these steps, other improvements have come, including a new school, increased income from tourism, and better health care. Raymond Rakotonindrina, from the forestry department, completes the story when he says:

"Now we're getting groups coming to us asking for parks. They can see the benefits of doing things this way."

FACT

Fewer than 1% of the estimated 125,000 flowering plant species in tropical forests have been examined closely for their possible use as human resources.

A forest full of wildlife is more valuable than a scorched desert. The wildlife that inhabits Madagascar's rain forests is among the rarest in the world.

Helping to preserve howler monkeys and other wildlife benefits people as well as animals.

Monkeys are a farmer's best friend

The area around the Belize River in Central America is a patchwork of farmland and young and mature forest. The forest is home to black howler monkeys—noisy, long-tailed primates who live in the treetops. Unfortunately, the farmers regarded the monkeys as pests who damaged their crops as they traveled between parts of the forest. Then a biologist came up with an idea to benefit both the farmers and the howler monkeys. He suggested that the farmers create a sanctuary for the monkeys by leaving strips of forest along the edges of their fields. This would provide food for the howlers and allow them to move through the forest without needing to cross the fields. The farmers were also encouraged to leave strips of forest along the river to reduce soil erosion and silting, and thus guarantee more fish for the villagers.

Costa Rica shows the way

The Guanacasta National Park is a small tropical forest in the lowlands of Costa Rica, in Central America. The plan there is to restore the park with the help of nearly 40,000 people who live around its borders. Farmers are employed to sow large areas with tree seeds and to plant seedlings, school and university students study the park's ecology and make field trips into the interior, and educational programs are run for local politicians and tourists. These activities bring money and jobs into the area, and the project also acts as a training ground in tropical forest management for scientists from all over the world. In this way, the scheme brings educational, environmental, and economic benefits to the region.

FACT

Today, over a hundred farmers take part in the Belize River Scheme, and the rain forest sanctuary supports about 1,100 black howler monkeys. The idea spread to seven other villages, and now about 6,000 tourists a year visit the area. The locals act as guides and provide accommodations. Everyone, including the howlers, benefits—earplugs are optional!

Ghana—fighting back?

In the African country of Ghana, over-logging, fire damage, demand for fuelwood, and shifting cultivation have meant the country's remaining rain forests are now designated as special conservation areas. Plans drawn up with the local people to protect the areas involve developing rain forest resources, such as fruit and craft products, outside the reserves. Friends of the Earth, Ghana, is working with Ashanti tribal villages to set up agro-forestry programs, which combine farming with forestry. Other conservation areas, such as sacred groves or holy places, traditional burial grounds, or areas protected by local laws, are managed by the local people.

School students visiting the Korup National Park in Cameroon. If people understand the rain forest and the benefits it brings, they will protect it.

These mahogany seedlings growing in Rondoñia, Brazil, will take decades to mature. But it is only by long-term planning that forests can be made sustainable.

Sustainable mahogany?

At present, there are few genuinely sustainable ways in which trees such as mahogany can be produced. Mahogany trees take a hundred years to reach the right size for logging, and no one wants to wait that long! In the Brazilian Amazon, an experiment is being run by the indigenous people themselves, the Xikrim of the Cateté River area, to see whether a solution is possible.

It began in 1996, when Indians and foresters worked together to plot every tree in an area of around 5,000 acres (2,000 ha) of rain forest. The area was then divided into separate plots called "parcels." In the first parcel, all the trees except for mahogany were removed, so that when the mahogany trees shed their seeds, only mahogany seedlings would grow in the clearings. The following year, the mature mahogany trees in the first parcel were harvested. In the same year, the non-mahogany species were removed from the next parcel, and so on. This process will continue year by year, so that while a continuous supply of mahogany can be harvested, new trees will gradually grow to replace them. In this way, the tribe will have a regular income and preserve their forest environment.

Learning lessons

It can be argued that these are isolated examples of sustainable development that only work in special circumstances. They also require large amounts of effort, in both financial and human terms, to maintain. But the real argument is not whether such schemes are worth pursuing, but whether the lessons and ideas learned from existing schemes can apply to the survival of the world's rain forests as a whole.

FACT

Over 80% of rain forest trees cut down in developing countries are for home use.

Pupil power: Students from a school in Chittoor District, India, tend a tree nursery. They have already reforested the valley in which the school stands.

VIEWPOINTS

"The survival of a species cannot simply hinge on the presence of armed guards. Perhaps, in the past, we have created this impression. Now we have to move wildlife management back into the community."
Claude Martin, Director-General, WWF International

"We cannot simply rely on the involvement of local communities in preserving wildlife. This is a situation where an ironfisted protectionist approach is needed."
John Watkin, African Conservation Centre, Nairobi

Do rain forests and people mix?

These examples raise another important question about making rain forests more sustainable. Do you make rain forests into massive parks from which as much human activity as possible is excluded? Or do you take the approach that rain forests and humans can and should exist together in harmony?

A transfer of power

In the past, the first approach has been adopted. For example, the Garamba National Park in north-east Democratic Republic of Congo is one of the last refuges of the wild northern white rhino. The park, made up of 1,235,000 acres (500,000 ha) of rain forest, is heavily fortified and patrolled by rangers who spend much of their time keeping people out and defending the rhinos against armed gangs of poachers.

Now all this is changing. The idea is to involve the local people, not to exclude them. The government is offering free fencing to help local farmers protect their crops, while encouraging

The horns that protect this wild northern white rhino from predators also create a target for poachers. But is it better to involve local people in their protection or employ armed guards and keep people away?

A fence keeps the elephant from trampling the crops. Many people believe that farming alongside wildlife is better than excluding people altogether.

them to live inside the park. In this way, the rhinos are less likely to be shot. Fostering a good relationship with local people may also encourage them to report poachers. This approach is being tested not just in Congo, but in Rwanda, the Central African Republic, and Southern Africa.

Not everyone agrees with this approach. Traditional conservationists argue that there is little evidence that sustainable management involving local people really works.

DEBATE

Inolving local people in the protection of their rain forest seems to make sense. But what are the pitfalls of this approach? What do you think is meant by "an ironfisted protectionist approach" (see viewpoint opposite), and how does it make you feel?

CAN THE RAIN FORESTS SURVIVE?

Ten Steps to Survival

Rain forests are now being protected in some encouraging ways, often with the involvement of local people. However, these are isolated examples, and change needs to take place on a much greater scale. Many people believe that if the rain forests are to have a realistic chance of survival, the following steps are necessary:

Protected rain forest in Australia. Do Earth's remaining rain forests have a realistic chance of survival?

1) Improving our knowledge of how much rain forest is left, how much is damaged, and to what degree. This means carrying out much more research.

2) Identifying those areas of forest richest in biodiversity and most endangered, and ensuring their rapid protection.

3) Slowing the flow of poor, landless people to rain forest areas. This means reducing poverty and providing the poor with a sustainable option for living in the forests.

4) Respecting the rights of forest peoples to continue living in traditional ways and on traditional land.

5) Rain forests should be valued not only for their economic importance. This means putting a real value on their biodiversity, their ability to

support the local people,
their medicinal value, their
influence on climate, and
their ability to protect soil
and water.

6) Pressure should be put on
banks and other organizations
to prevent money from being
lent for environmentally
destructive projects. This
includes road-building
through forest areas and the
construction of large dams.

*A slum on the edge of a swamp in Rio
de Janeiro, Brazil. Reducing poverty
worldwide is one answer to the
problem of rain forest destruction.*

7) Logging companies should regenerate felled
areas. Logging methods should be modified
so that only selected trees are harvested and
removed, with as little damage as possible.

8) Farming, tree/crop plantations, and
ranching should be concentrated in forest
areas that have already been cleared,
followed by the sustainable management
of these areas to allow them to recover.

9) Existing forests should be protected by
working hand-in-hand with local people;
farmers should receive help and training
to introduce them to less destructive
farming methods.

10) The international community should work
together to reforest and repair areas and soil
affected by deforestation.

These are fine ideas, but they will only be
successful if the countries involved realize that
it is in their interests to protect their resources;
by making the rain forests profitable for them.

Making the rain forests pay

Countries are far more likely to protect their rain forests if there are better alternatives to logging, farming, and other forms of destruction. For example, it has been shown that traditional, nondestructive uses of the rain forest, such as tapping wild rubber, harvesting fruit, oils, and medicinal plants, can produce a much greater income than logging, shifting agriculture, or cattle ranching. One study carried out in Peru, South America, showed that these uses produced seven times as much income per acre as heavy logging.

Farming and forests

The Maya Indians of Chiapas, Mexico, carry out agroforestry, a very efficient form of farming. A number of different crops are grown at the same

Agroforestry means the forest pays for itself. Different crops are grown on a small patch of land within this forest in Nigeria. Later, this piece of land will be left to regrow.

time on a single plot of land among trees that are a mixture of fruit and fuel trees. This allows up to 75 different crop species to be cultivated on a single acre for up to seven years. In this way, one farmer clears fewer than 25 acres (10 ha) of forest in a lifetime, rather than hundreds of acres using the traditional "slash-and-burn" method. Agroforestry is also used by the Chagga people of Mount Kilimanjaro in Africa and the Lua of Thailand. Because it allows farmers to stay on the land without having to move on, the destructive "land hunger" is removed.

Living with logging

Logging does not need to be destructive. We have seen that it is a valuable resource if managed sustainably. In 1993, a group of nongovernment organizations, scientists, indigenous people, and representatives of the logging industry formed an alliance called the Forest Stewardship Council (FSC). Their aim was to promote forestry that would not destroy rain forests but would benefit local people and the economy of the country. Now it is possible to buy tropical timber bearing the FSC logo, which means that it has come from a sustainable source. Now many countries, including Sweden, Brazil, and even Indonesia, are developing national plans based on the FSC standards.

Ecotourism

Another way of making rain forests financially successful is to encourage visitors, or eco-tourists, from other countries to pay to enjoy visiting them. In the 1960s and 1970s, much of Costa Rica's rain forest was cleared to graze cattle for sale to the United States and Europe. In the mid-1970s, Costa Rica set up a system of national parks that now protects 12 percent of its land, half of which is reserved for the indigenous people. Today, income from ecotourism is the country's major source of outside income.

This logo stands for Forest Stewardship Council. It means that this wood has been obtained from a sustainable source. Buying wood bearing this logo means contributing to the survival of rain forests.

What can we do?

"No man made a greater mistake than he who did nothing because he thought he could only do a little."
Henry Thoreau: writer and philosopher

Many of the actions required in the fight to save the rain forests need the cooperation and involvement of governments and international bodies such as the United Nations. However, individual action can also make a difference.

Look at the quotation at the top of this page. What do you think this means? The history of the human race is full of examples of people who have achieved a great deal through seemingly small actions. A few years ago, a big petroleum company wanted to sink a disused oil exploration platform off the Scottish coast. The local people were outraged and took action by protesting to politicians, writing to newspapers, signing petitions, and refusing to buy the company's gas. Finally, the company agreed to consider dismantling the platform safely on land and recycling the parts.

An ecological home in Denmark built from recycled materials and equipped with energy-saving devices. Less general pressure on the environment means that the rain forests will benefit.

Making a difference

There are many ways in which individuals can help conserve the rain forests, including buying wood certified by the FSC and products such as tea and coffee, grown sustainably in tropical countries where the farmers are paid a fair price for them.

You can also buy soaps and shampoos made from rain forest products where it is the indigenous people who benefit from the sale and not a large corporation. Ask your local council if they run a wood recycling project (old wood from demolished buildings is often burned), and if the answer is "no," lobby for one. Join organizations that campaign for rain forests and other endangered habitats and organize fund-raising events in schools.

Thinking differently

But most important of all, we need to change our attitude toward the world and try to live with the Earth in mind. We must understand that everything we do is in some way connected to the future of the planet, including the rain forests.

Ecotourism, such as in this example in a Belize rain forest, brings greater financial benefits than selling the rain forest's timber. Even here there are dangers, however, if the tourists cause too much damage or disturbance.

VIEWPOINTS

"Whether industrialized or not, we all have but one lifeboat (the Earth). No more than a few decades remain before the chance to prevent the threats that confront us will be lost."
Letter to the world's leaders by 1,680 leading scientists, 1992

"In 20 to 30 years' time, today's children will be running the world. If they understand the importance of their environment, they are more likely to protect and sustain it."
Professor Daniel Janzen, Forest Project Leader

Will the rain forests survive?

"We abuse land because we regard it as a commodity belonging to us. When we see land as a community to which we belong, we may begin to use it with love and respect."
Aldo Leopold: environmentalist and writer

A lost cause?

The plight of the world's rain forests is very serious. A number of scientists believe that saving much of the rain forests in countries like Indonesia and Brazil is no longer possible. No doubt some specially protected areas will remain in these regions, but it will be not be enough to preserve the enormous biodiversity, or to save the indigenous people that these rain forests once supported. These scientists believe that the only way forward is to concentrate on other areas in the world where destruction is less advanced. This might include Papua New Guinea, parts of Africa such as the Democratic Republic of Congo, and the Central Amazon Basin.

Or cause for hope?

Other scientists are less pessimistic. They believe that the tide is turning and that governments worldwide are beginning to recognize the damage they will do to their own economies, their land, and their people if they do not control forest destruction.

Read the quotation at the top of this page about our attitude toward the land. Does it sound over-sentimental? It must be difficult to love and respect the land when it is turning to dust under your feet. However, perhaps we are missing the point. We know that it is possible to live in harmony with rain forests—"the land"—as many indigenous people have done so for thousands of years.

No easy answers

It is clear that there are no easy solutions and that some solutions may well bring more problems. For example, ecotourism can disrupt indigenous people's lives, while building hotels or using tourist vehicles may cause environmental damage. Planting more trees will certainly help to feed the hunger for timber and soak up excess carbon dioxide, but growing a rain forest takes thousands, possibly millions, of years.

A sustainable future?

Whatever happens, the only sensible way forward is to opt for a sustainable future. Healthy, widespread, and vital rain forests will support far more of humanity than lifeless deserts or exhausted cattle ranches. To achieve this will take a huge amount of cooperation, money and time.

Cooperation can be achieved if there is enough will. Money can come from the rich, developed countries who have benefited from destroying their own forests in the past and who still benefit from the destruction of rain forests today. The only real shortfall we have is time.

> **DEBATE**
>
> Is it really too late? Is it acceptable that rain forests may, in your lifetime, be preserved only in special parks or in certain parts of the world? What, if anything, can individuals do to prevent this? Can young people have a voice and, if so, how can they express it?

We belong to the world, the world does not belong to us. Therefore we have a responsibility to protect it—and that includes the rain forests.

GLOSSARY

agroforestry combining agriculture with forestry, harvesting both crops and trees.

biodiversity the variety of plants and animals inhabiting an area or country. A high biodiversity usually indicates a rich and healthy environment.

buffer zone a region around a specially protected area where some development is allowed to shield the protected area from outside influences.

conservation any action taken that conserves (protects) the environment.

conservationist a person, often a scientist, who supports the idea of conservation.

conversion land cleared rain forest land designated for agricultural use.

developed countries wealthy, highly industrialized countries, such as the U.K., U.S., and Japan, who often use resources wastefully.

developing countries countries in the process of developing, often from a largely rural (agricultural) way of life.

development the way in which a country develops its resources; for example, its industry, health services, and education system.

ecosystem a community of plants, animals, and their environment that is interdependent.

ecotourism tourism that uses the environment to attract foreign visitors.

exports the products a country sells abroad.

fertilizers natural or artificial nutrients added to the soil to increase its fertility.

global warming changes in world climate caused by activities such as burning fossil fuels, resulting in unusual weather patterns.

greenhouse gases gases produced by activities such as burning fossil fuels, which

contribute to global climate change (global warming).

hardwood timber that comes from a broad-leaved deciduous tree as opposed to an evergreen tree, such as a conifer.

hydroelectric power electricity produced by harnessing the energy of water.

immigrants people who move into an area from another country or area, often as a result of poverty or unfair treatment.

imports the products a country buys from abroad.

indigenous people the original inhabitants of an area or country.

mineral/timber rights the rights bought by a company, sometimes from another country, which allow them to set up mining or logging activities in a particular area.

monsoon a season of heavy rain in a tropical country, such as Bangladesh.

poachers people who kill animals illegally either for their own use or to sell.

recycling turning unwanted material, such as wood or old newspapers, into new products.

reforestation planting trees to replace destroyed forests. Although important, these new forests will not have such great biodiversity as the original forests.

shifting cultivation a method of farming poor soil, where a cleared area is cultivated for a few years and then abandoned.

softwood timber that comes from an evergreen or coniferous tree and is more easily sawed.

sustainable using resources such as forests, minerals, or land so that they supply people with what they need without damaging supplies for future generations.

World Bank an international organization that administers economic aid among member countries.

BOOKS, CDS, AND VIDEOS

Students may find the following books, CDs, and videos useful:

BOOKS:
Lyman, Francesca (compiler), American Museum of Natural History. *Inside the Dzanga-Sangha Rain Forest: Exploring the Heart of Central Africa*. Workman, 1998.

Morgan, Sally. *Saving the Rain Forest*. Franklin Watts, 1999.

Parker, Edward, and Anna Lewington. *People of the Rain Forests*. Raintree Steck-Vaughn, 1998.

Senior, Kathryn, *Rain Forest*. Franklin Watts, 1999.

Thomas, Rob. *Green Thumb*. Simon & Schuster Juvenile, 1999.

CDs:
Baker, Lucy, and Jason Page. *Rain Forests*. Two-Can Publishers, 2000.

VIDEOS:
The Kayapo—Indians of the Brazilian Rain Forest, 1987.

National Geographic's Rain Forest, 1983.

National Geographic's Rain Forest: Heroes of the High Frontier, 1999.

USEFUL ADDRESSES

www.rain forest-alliance.org
Gives information about the New York-based Rain
Forest Alliance organization and its activities, including
information on recent conservation projects. Includes
material for teachers and pupils.

www.eelink.net/eeactivties-rain forests.html
Produced by the North American Association for
Environmental Education. This site lists educational
activities related to rain forests.

www.eduweb.com/amazon.html
Learn about the rain forest and its people through this
interactive site. Explores the geography of the Amazon
through online games and activities.

www.rain forests.net
Gives latest information about rain forest clearance and
related issues such as poverty, population, and number
of extinctions; gives figures for past and future. Links to
other sites on different environmental issues.

www.wrm.org.uy
Website of the World Rain Forest Movement; gives
information on rain forests by region and country,
including organizations and publications. A useful
information source.

www.globaleye.org.uk
Based on the magazine Global Eye produced
for schools by Worldaware on behalf of the Department
for International Development (DFID). Includes
information and activities on a range of global issures
including deforestation and poverty.

www.globaldimension.org.uk
Part of the National Grid for Learning. Includes
support materials on all aspects of global learning,
including a database of educational resources, school
linking and interactive elements.

UNITED STATES
Friends of the Earth International
1025 Vermont Avenue N.W.
Washington, DC 20005
Tel: 202-783-7400
www.foe.org/international

Greenpeace USA
Greenpeace USA
702 H Street N.W., Suite 300
Washington, DC 2001
Tel: 202-462-1177
www.greenpeace.org

Rainforest Action Network
221 Pine Street, Suite 500
San Francisco, CA 94104
415-398-4404
www.ran.org

World Wildlife Fund
1250 Twenty-Fourth Street, N.W.
P. O. Box 97180
Washington, DC 20037
Tel: 1-800-CALL-WWF
www.worldwildlife.org

CANADA
WWF Canada
245 Eglinton Avenue East, Suite 410
Toronto, Ontario
Canada M4P 3J1
Tel: 1-800-26-PANDA
   1-416-489-8800
   1-416-489-3611
www.wwfcanada.org

INDEX

Page numbers in **bold** refer to illustrations.

agriculture *see* farming
agroforestry 47, **54**, 54–5
Amazon region 4, **6**, 7, 11, 24, 28, 30, 31,
   35, 36, **40**, 48, 58

Bangladesh **6**, 12, 30
Belize **10**, 46, 47, **57**
biodiversity 10–11, 27, 28, 52, 53, 58
Borneo **6**, **7**, 8–9, 10, 21
Brazil **5**, **6**, **8**, 10, 16, 18, 21, 26, 28, 29, 30,
   30, 31, 35, 37, 42, **42**, 48, **53**, 55, 58

cattle ranching 8, **20**, 21, 28, 40, 53, 54, 55
Central African Republic **6**, 51
Congo, Democratic Republic of **6**, 10, 31,
   50–51, 58
conservation groups 11, 19, 23, 27, 38, 39,
   47, 50–51, 55
conservation schemes 38, 44–51
Costa Rica **6**, 10, 47, 55

dams 22–23, 53
diseases 22, 29, 31, 36–37

Earth Summit (1992) 42, 43, **43**
endangered species **10**, 10–11, 38, 39, **39**,
   50, 50–51
European Union 25

farming 5, **7**, 8-9, 16, 18, 20, 21, 26, 32, 40,
   41, 46, 47, 50-51, 53, 54–55
fires *see* rain forests, burning of
food 13, 15, **15**, 16, 17, 24, 28, 29, 31
Forestry Stewardship Council 55, **55**, 56
French Guiana **6**, 22, **36**

fuelwood 8, 30–31, **31**, 40

Ghana **6**, 47
global warming 12–13
Guatemala **6**, 15

hydroelectric power 22–23

India **6**, 21, 22, 23, 38, 39, **49**
indigenous peoples 5, 13, 14, 28, **34**, 34–39,
   41, 52, 53, 55, 57, 58
   Arara 29
   Ashanti 47
   Chagga 55
   Dayak 8–9, 19
   Kayapo 29
   Lua 55
   Maya 54–55
   Menyah **7**
   Penan 5, **34**, 35
   Surui **29**
   Talang Mamak **17**
   Tikuna 35
   Xikrim 48
   Yanomami 37, **37**
Indonesia 4, **6**, 8–9, 16, **18–19**, 18–21, 26,
   32–33, 55
industry 22–25, 30, **30**
international community, role of 15, 23, 25,
   27, 30, 32, 33, 41, 42–43, 53, 55, 56
Ivory Coast **6**, 15, 26

Japan **6**, 25, 27, 35, 42

logging 7, 8, 9, 26–29, 32, **32**, 35, 38, 41, 48,
   53, 54, 55
   illegal **4**, 28, 29, 32–33, **33**

Madagascar **6**, **14**, **38**, 44–45, **44–45**
mahogany **26**, 28, **48**, 48–49,
Malaysia **6**, 26, 35
medicines **14**, 14–15, 53, 54
mercury poisoning 24–25, 29
Mexico **6**, 15, 54–55
minerals 5, 8, 24, 25
mining **23**, **24**, 24–25, 29, 32, **36**, 36–37, 40, **40**, **41**

national parks 4, 39, 44–45, 47, **47**, 50–51, 55
nature reserves 10, 46, 47
Nigeria 31, **54**

Papua New Guinea **6**, 26, 58
Peru **4**, **6**, 54
Philippines **6**, 26
plantations 8, 9, 17, 20, 27, 32, 40, 41, 53
population growth 41
poverty 5, 8–9, 17, 19, 27, 29, 31, 33, 35, 41, 52, 53

rain forest destruction 4, **8**, **18–19**, 18–21, 22, **26**, 28, 36
    attempts to prevent 32, 44–51, 54–57
    causes of 5, 8-9, 16, 18, 21, 22, 24, 26, 30, 32, 40–41
    effects of 5, 7, 11, 13, 15, 19, 27, 36
    rate of 6, 7, **9**, 27
rain forests
    Amazon *see* Amazon region
    animals 5, 10–11, **10–11**, 15, **45**, **46**, 46, 47
    burning of 8, 9, 16, **18–19**, 18–21

chances of survival 5, 52–53, 58–59
climate **4**, 12–13, 53
habitats 4, 10–11, **44–46**
location of 6, **6**
peoples *see* indigenous peoples
plants **4**, 5, 10, 13, **14**, 14–15, 26–28, 45
products 13, 15, **15**, 47, 54, 56, 57
timber 5, 8, 15, **26–28**, 26–29, 32–33, 40, 44–45, 54, 55, 56
Rio Declaration on Environment and Development 40, 42, 43
roads **5**, 8, 24, 26, 27, 28, **28**, 29, 53
Rwanda **6**, 10, 31, 51

Savii (Western Samoa) 38
settlement programs 16, 21, 29, 35
settlers 16, **16**, 18, 20, 21, 26, 27, 28, 52
shifting cultivation 18, 54
slash-and-burn agriculture 8, 18, 41
soil **4**, 17, 18, 53
    erosion 8, 12, **13**, 21, 24, 46, 53
Sumatra **6**, 11, **16**, **17**, 19, **33**
sustainable development 42–51, 53, 54–57, 59

Thailand **6**, **27**, 30, 55
tourism 45, 47, 55, **57**, 59

United Kingdom 28
United States 21, 28, 55

Venezuela **6**, 28, 37

World Bank 23, 25, 30, 33